Ancient Persian Warfare

By Phyllis G. Jestice

Please visit our web site at www.garethstevens.com
For a free color catalog describing Gareth Stevens Publishing's
list of high-quality books call 1-800-542-2595 (USA)
or 1-800-387-3187 (Canada).
Gareth Stevens Publishing's fax: 1-877-542-2596

Library of Congress Cataloging-in-Publication Data

Jestice, Phyllis G.
    Ancient Persian Warfare / by Phyllis G. Jestice.
        p. cm. — (Ancient Warfare)
    Includes bibliographical references and index.
    ISBN-10: 1-4339-1973-7   (lib. bdg.)
    ISBN-13: 978-1-4339-1973-2   (lib. bdg.)
    1. Military art and science—Iran—History—To 1500—Juvenile literature.
    2. Iran—History, Military—Juvenile literature.   3. Iran—History—To 640—
Juvenile literature.   4. Military art and science—History—To 500—Juvenile literature.
    5. Military history, Ancient—Juvenile literature. I. Title.
    U31.J475   2009
    355.020935—DC22   2009006199

This North American edition first published in 2010 by
GS Learning Library
1 Reader's Digest Road
Pleasantville, NY 10570-7000 USA

Copyright © 2010 by Amber Books, Ltd.
Produced by Amber Books Ltd., Bradley's Close
74–77 White Lion Street
London N1 9PF, U.K.

Amber Project Editor: James Bennett
Amber Designer: Joe Conneally

Gareth Stevens Executive Managing Editor: Lisa M. Herrington
Gareth Stevens Editor: Joann Jovinelly
Gareth Stevens Senior Designer: Keith Plechaty

Interior Images
All illustrations © Amber Books, Ltd., except:
AKG Images: 9 (Electa), 12 (Erich Lessing); Art Archive: 4 (Gianni Dagli Orti/British Museum),
16, 20 (Gianni Dagli Orti); Bridgeman Art Library: 3, 13 (Alinari/Museo Archeologico Nazionale,
Naples), 14 (Ken Welsh), 23 (Giraudon); Corbis: 8 (Wolfgang Kaehler), 29 (Art Archive);
De Agostini Picture Library: 5 (N. Cirani), 21 (C. Sappa), 22; Dorling Kindersley: 11 (Alistair Duncan);
Mary Evans Picture Library: 15, 19 (AISA Media)

Cover Images
Front Cover: Left, Achaemenid relief sculpture of an archer (Burstein Collection/Corbis); top right,
gold plaque from the Oxus treasure (Photos.com); bottom right, ancient Greek depiction of a Persian
archer (AISA Media/Mary Evans Picture Library)
Back Cover: Center, parchment (James Steidl/Dreamstime); right, Persian marine (Amber Books)

Printed in the United States of America

1 2 3 4 5 6 7 8 9 13 12 11 10 09

Contents

CHAPTER 1

Foot Soldiers

Persia was the first great **empire** in the world. From about 550 B.C. until 330 B.C., it spanned the region now known as the Middle East as well as parts of North Africa, Asia, and Europe. The Persian **Achaemenid** (Uh-KEM-uh-nid) **Empire** stretched from Libya and Egypt in the west to India in the east. It took in all or parts of what is now Israel, Cyprus, Turkey, Syria, Jordan, Lebanon, Iran, Iraq, Greece, Afghanistan, and Pakistan.

In this sculpture, enemies of the Assyrians are shown impaled on poles.

▼ ASSYRIAN WARFARE
Before the rise of the Persian Empire, the region now known as the Middle East was controlled by the Assyrians, a violent, warlike people. Like the Persians, their foot soldiers fought with bows and arrows.

The Assyrians developed siege machines, like this battering ram.

A Mighty Empire

Before the rise of the Achaemenid Empire, the Persians lived in southern Persia (present-day Iran). The **Medes** ruled the land to the north. The Persians mostly lived in settlements or traveled from place to place as **nomads**, or wandering tribes. That changed when the Persian leader Cyrus the Great (Cyrus II) fought the Medes for their territory. He united northern and southern Persia as one kingdom. That union marked the start of the Achaemenid Empire.

Throughout its history, the Achaemenid Empire had several kings. Two leaders led the empire during its time of greatest power. The first king, Cyrus the Great, ruled from 559 to 529 B.C. The other king, Darius the Great (Darius I), ruled from 522 to 486 B.C. Darius founded Persepolis, the Persian capital city and seat of power for the Achaemenid kings. Persepolis took more than a century to build. It was a **fortress** that contained magnificent palaces and huge halls.

▼ THE RUINS OF PERSEPOLIS
This photograph shows all that is left of Persepolis, the great city of the Persian kings. The Greek leader Alexander the Great (356–323 B.C.) burned it to the ground in 330 B.C. He sought revenge for the Persians' earlier capture of Athens.

The Empire Expands

As ancient Persia thrived, its territory grew. The Persians built wealth by trading goods with foreign kingdoms. Trading took place in towns along the **Silk Road**. That was a system of land and sea routes that ran from the Mediterranean Sea across Central Asia to China.

As time passed, progress was made. Water for drinking and farming was brought to dry desert areas through wells and underground channels. Art and architecture thrived. Great palaces were built. Gold and silver were made into bowls, jewelry, and other ornaments. Kings and nobles hosted festive banquets with a bounty of food and wine.

Persians made their official language **Aramaic**. They also produced currency in the form of coins. **Zoroastrianism**, a new religion, became the official Persian faith, but other religions were allowed.

Eventually, the empire was divided into twenty **satrapies**, or provinces. Each province had its own **satrap**, or governor. The satrap maintained law and order and took charge of the military. Royal inspectors toured each satrapy and reported back to the king.

Foot Soldiers

All Persian men served in the army. Soldiers supplied their own weapons.

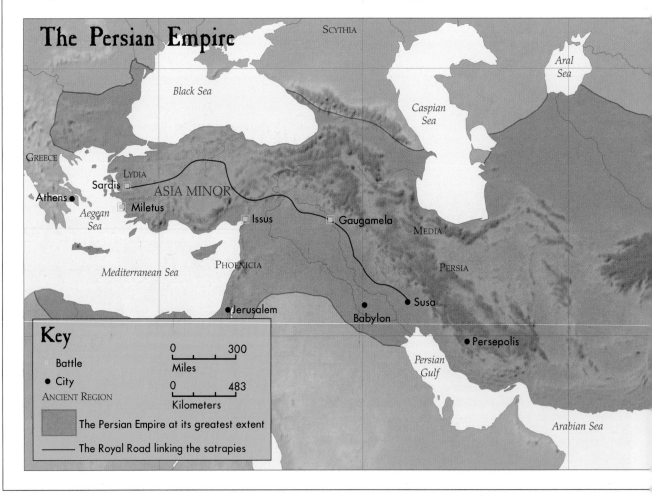

The Persian Empire

SCYTHIA

Aral Sea

Black Sea

Caspian Sea

GREECE

LYDIA

Sardis

ASIA MINOR

Athens

Aegean Sea

Miletus

Issus

Gaugamela

MEDIA

PERSIA

Mediterranean Sea

PHOENICIA

Jerusalem

Babylon

Susa

Persepolis

Persian Gulf

Arabian Sea

Key

☐ Battle

● City

ANCIENT REGION

0 — 300 Miles

0 — 483 Kilometers

The Persian Empire at its greatest extent

—— The Royal Road linking the satrapies

Since it was less expensive to fight on foot than on horseback, most men were foot soldiers. Even though the Persian army was large, it was disorganized. Because the soldiers had trained in different places, they had different fighting methods. For example, the Persian army sometimes had **archers** from Persia, spearmen from Egypt, and **slingers** from Palestine.

The Persian kings kept a small standing army that was well trained and well organized. Greek historians tell us that this elite part of the army was divided into units of 10, 100, and 1,000. Those men had better armor and were more willing to fight. When there was no war, they guarded fortresses.

Few soldiers from the larger army wanted to fight for Persia. Some came from lands that had been conquered by Persia and forced into its empire. Because those men were not Persian, they did not want to risk their lives for Persia. In fact, Persian commanders sometimes stood behind troops and whipped them until they advanced against the enemy.

The Greeks

The Persian armies, numbering in the thousands, fought the armies of neighboring cultures, such as the **Lydians** and **Babylonians**. The Persians often won, absorbing more territory into their empire.

The Greek soldiers, however, were better fighters than Persia's other foreign enemies. Unlike the Persians, Greek foot soldiers believed in face-to-face fighting.

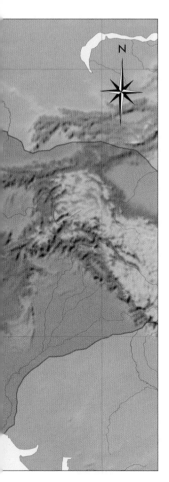

◄ THE PERSIAN EMPIRE UNDER DARIUS I
The enormous Persian Empire reached its natural boundary by 500 B.C. There were mountain ranges to the east, deserts to the south, and bare grasslands to the north.

They moved in close to the enemy and jabbed them with spears instead of releasing arrows from a distance. The Greeks were able to fight well in close combat. Their heavy armor, shields, and helmets protected them.

The Persian foot soldiers' arrows caused few injuries to the armored Greek soldiers. In Greece, for instance, at the battle of Thermopylae (Ther-MOP-ill-ee) in 480 B.C., just a few hundred Greeks stopped thousands of Persian soldiers. The standoff lasted for several days. After losing thousands of men, the Persians only made it across the mountains by finding a path that took them behind the Greeks. Once there, the Persians attacked the Greeks from both sides, winning the battle. The Persians then moved southeast into Athens, and burned it to the ground. But the Greeks held their territory. The Greek Empire did not fall to a Persian conquest.

At the battle of Marathon in 490 B.C., the Greeks proved that their

◄ **ANCIENT BATTLE SITE**
After 2,500 years have passed, it is hard to imagine that this was the site where the battle of Thermopylae took place. The Persian army met the Greek soldiers at the bottom of the cliff at a narrow path about 100 feet (30 meters) wide.

weapons were far more advanced than Persian weapons. The Greeks ran forward to close the distance between the two armies. The Persians were doomed. They had only light shields and no armor. More than 6,000 Persian soldiers died that day, compared to only 192 Greeks.

The Persians needed heavier armor, but metal was expensive. The Persians also needed more training. Persian kings began paying Greek foot soldiers to do the heavy fighting in their armies. That solution worked well—until the Persians faced Alexander the Great. His soldiers wore armor and helmets. He also knew how to organize and inspire them better than any general had before.

▶ **SCYTHIAN WARRIORS**
The Persians fought several wars against the Scythians (SI-thee-uns). A Scythian soldier is seen on this gold jug stringing his bow. This artifact was found in a Scythian tomb in present-day Ukraine.

CHAPTER 2

Fighting with Horses

The main Scythian weapon was a small, powerful bow.

The archer carried a **quiver** of arrows where he could reach them easily.

Scythians did not use horseshoes, so they had to be careful not to ride their horses on rough ground.

◄ A SCYTHIAN HORSE ARCHER
Scythians grew up with their horses. They learned to ride as soon as they could walk. Their light, quick horses were highly trained, leaving the archer's hands free to use his weapons.

Early Persian armies had few mounted soldiers. Cyrus the Great knew how useful mounted soldiers could be, as two of his greatest enemies used **cavalry** in battle. One Persian enemy, the Lydians, was from western Anatolia (present-day Turkey). Cyrus developed a clever plan to defeat the Lydian cavalry, or soldiers on horseback. At the battle of Sardis in 547 B.C., Cyrus took all the camels from his **caravan** and put them in front of his army. (Horses hate the smell of camels.) At the battle, the Lydian horses tried to keep away from the camels, but it was no use. The Lydian horsemen were forced to fight on foot, making it easier for the Persians to defeat them.

Another Persian enemy, the Scythians, also relied on horsemen. That group lived to the north of Persia, mostly as wandering nomads. The

Scythians were expert horsemen, and Cyrus failed to defeat them. He attacked the Scythians in 530 B.C. and died in the fight.

Persian Light Cavalry

After Cyrus' death, the Persians made cavalry a part of their army. Persian cavalry was posted on the outer wings of the troops. With cavalry covering the sides, archers in the center could shoot repeatedly. After the archers fired all their arrows, the horsemen rode in to kill anyone left standing.

Early Persian cavalry did not wear armor. They threw **javelins** or shot small bows from horseback. Their horses were small. The tallest horses stood only about 52 inches (132 centimeters) high at the shoulder. Small horses were useful because they could move quickly. They were not meant for fighting in close combat.

Ancient "Knights"

Cyrus the Great lost his final battle against the mounted Scythians because body armor and helmets protected them. The Scythians carried spears and fought in close combat. Heavy cavalry, the "knights" of the ancient world, terrified unarmored Persian foot soldiers. The force of the speeding cavalry broke up close ranks. That force also helped Scythian riders strike even harder with their spears, making them deadlier. Whenever Darius the Great conquered armies that used heavy cavalry, he quickly made them part of the Persian army.

DID YOU KNOW?

The Persians invented a system of delivering messages over vast distances. A horseback rider traveled until he reached a station where he and his horse could rest. Then, another rider and horse took over. That chain continued until the message was delivered.

◄ A SURPRISING WEAPON
Few camels were used in battle because they were hard to control and often disrupted cavalry. Cyrus the Great used camels as a surprise weapon at the battle of Sardis in 547 B.C.

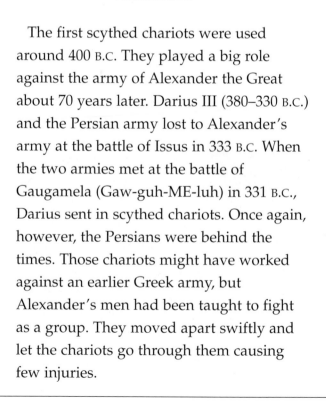

▶ **PERSIANS VERSUS GREEKS**
This Greek vase shows a
Persian cavalryman attacking a
Greek foot soldier. In a real
battle the Greek soldier would
have worn heavy armor. The
painting shows clearly the
difference between the fighting
styles of those two enemies.

The Persian uses a
light thrusting spear.

Persian horses were
small, but the artist
painted the horse on
this ancient vase to
appear even smaller!

A Strange Experiment

The Persians built their empire after the age
of chariots, but putting soldiers on horseback
was a less expensive way to use horses.
Persian generals had to think of a way to
fight against—and break up—tight lines of
Greek foot soldiers, so their arrows could hit
their targets. Their answer was the **scythed
chariot**. That was an ancient war chariot, but
with one difference. Each scythed chariot
had long swords attached to its wheels. The
driver rode toward the enemy. The horses
shoved foot soldiers to the side, and the
spinning blades chopped off the arms and
legs of anyone who got too close. Scythed
chariots were horribly frightening. The
Persians were helped by the disorder caused
by the panic of enemy soldiers.

The first scythed chariots were used
around 400 B.C. They played a big role
against the army of Alexander the Great
about 70 years later. Darius III (380–330 B.C.)
and the Persian army lost to Alexander's
army at the battle of Issus in 333 B.C. When
the two armies met at the battle of
Gaugamela (Gaw-guh-ME-luh) in 331 B.C.,
Darius sent in scythed chariots. Once again,
however, the Persians were behind the
times. Those chariots might have worked
against an earlier Greek army, but
Alexander's men had been taught to fight
as a group. They moved apart swiftly and
let the chariots go through them causing
few injuries.

The Battle of Gaugamela

After losing the battle of Issus to Alexander the Great, Darius III spent a long time putting together another army. Finally the two armies met again near the village of Gaugamela, which historians think may have been in Iraq. Darius' men had cleared the ground so he could use his terrifying scythed chariots. The Persian soldiers also had better weapons to fight the Greeks. Darius had even brought in 15 war elephants that were trained in India. That was a first in Persian warfare. Darius placed the elephants in the front and center of the battlefield to frighten the enemy.

The Persian army outnumbered the Greeks by five or six to one. But Darius had not planned on Alexander's military genius. On that front, the battle was lost before it had begun.

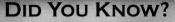

DID YOU KNOW?

Alexander the Great captured Darius III's mother after the battle of Issus. She apparently liked her new "son" better than her old one. When she heard of Darius III's death, she said, "I have only one son, [Alexander], and he is king of all Persia."

◀ **DARIUS III AT GAUGAMELA**
This detail of a mosaic was discovered at Pompeii, the Roman town buried by volcanic ash in A.D. 79. It shows Darius III in his chariot, turning to flee as Alexander the Great approaches with his cavalry.

13

CHAPTER 3

Weapons and Armor

Persian warfare did not include hand-to-hand fighting, so Persian soldiers had little equipment. They fought with light weapons. That was natural in the warm climate of the Middle East, where the hot summers could be as much of a threat as enemy soldiers.

Because of the heat, many Persian soldiers did not wear armor. Armor was also heavy and the metal used to make it was very expensive—something that few men could afford. At most, a soldier might have a **tunic** made of padded linen. That was enough to stop arrows from piercing skin.

▼ **IN THE HEAT OF BATTLE**
This painting from 1920 shows the battle of Issus, at the moment when King Darius III turned his chariot and fled from Alexander the Great. In the heat of the Middle East, both sides are depicted without helmets, wearing only cloth tunics.

▲ PERSIAN FIGHTERS

These are soldiers from Elam, part of the Persian Empire. They are armed with spears, bows, and arrows. Note that they do not wear body armor.

Soldiers also carried large rectangular shields about five feet (1.52 meters) high. Those light shields were made of thin sticks woven together and often backed with animal skins. They were little use against a spear, but they protected against most arrows. Often, shield-bearers stood with large shields in front of a row of archers, while the archers shot over their heads.

▶ **THE 10,000 IMMORTALS**
The likenesses of members of the Persian Royal Guard—the 10,000 Immortals—were carved as relief sculptures to decorate the royal court at Persepolis. They were the only Persian soldiers who wore metal armor in battle.

Only the best-armed foot soldiers—the 10,000 Immortals who guarded the king—wore iron **breastplates**. But even they used shields woven from thin sticks.

Unlike typical foot soldiers, horsemen were rich nobles. They could afford to buy protective armor. The heavy cavalry wore metal helmets and armor that covered them at least from neck to waist. Sometimes their horses also wore armor.

A Rain of Arrows

One reason Persia became a great empire was that it had the best archers. Years earlier, around 600 B.C., Persian kings brought Scythian archers to Persia from the north to teach young men how to shoot. Years of practice followed.

When preparing for a battle, Persian generals set up groups of troops with archers in their centers. Together the archers

◀ A SCYTHIAN WARRIOR
Their defeats at the hands of the Scythians inspired the Persian kings to hire Scythian archers. That changed the Persian army into a force that depended heavily on archery.

Arrows were made of reed with stone tips.

Compound bows were made from layers of wood, horn, and animal tendons glued together.

Most Scythians serving in the Persian army wore pants.

This picture of two typical
Persian foot soldiers is
copied from an ancient
Persian wall carving. The
men fought as partners. The
spearman protected himself
and his partner with his
shield, so the archer had
both hands free to use
his bow.

Persian shields were
made of simple woven
reeds, sometimes with a
cover of animal hide.
They were strong
enough to defend
against most arrows, but
not all Greek spears.

Unlike the Scythians, the
Persians used a simple
bow made from one
piece of wood strung
with cord.

The only advantage
the Persians had in
their armor over the
Greeks' armor was
their strong boots.

shot arrow after arrow at enemy soldiers
who usually wore little body armor. Most
enemies were wounded or killed in the first
wave of battle. After the archers shot their
arrows, slingers fired stones or small lead
balls into the enemy from a closer range.
The general then sent in cavalry.

Foot soldiers were the last men to enter
the battle. Their job was to kill or capture
men who were wounded. Foot soldiers were

poorly equipped. Some had spears or short
swords, but they did not wear armor.
Persian foot soldiers did not fight in hand-
to-hand combat.

Weapons

Most Persian soldiers were too poor to
have good weapons. Early Persian bows
were made from long pieces of springy
wood that were bent into curves with

string. Those were much less powerful than later bows made of horn and animal tendons. Persian arrows were light, with bronze tips. Most foot soldiers used spears—long wooden poles with metal heads. Some Persian foot soldiers also had daggers to use as back-up weapons. A few may have had short swords called **akinakes**. Those had wide, heavy blades and looked like modern machetes. Akinakes were deadly. One Persian king died after stabbing himself accidentally with his own sword while climbing onto his horse.

▶ **A PERSIAN ARCHER**
Much of what we know about Persian weapons and armor comes from Greek art, such as this detail of a cup from around 500 B.C. But historians must use care when interpreting the meaning of ancient works of art. For instance, the Greeks often depicted their Persian enemies as **barbarians**.

CHAPTER 4

Great Leaders

The ancient Persians' two great warrior kings were Cyrus the Great (Cyrus II, 580–529 B.C.) and Darius the Great (Darius I, 522–486 B.C.). Kings had generals, but the kings themselves led their armies. Soldiers often fought harder when led by their king, but not all kings were skilled leaders. Persian kings were not chosen because of their fighting abilities. Some were poor military leaders, such as Xerxes I (519–465 B.C.) or Darius III.

Cyrus the Great

Cyrus started as king of a small territory. Over time, he drew his people together and defeated the Medes. Cyrus also defeated the Babylonians, the Lydians, and several other cultures. There was no secret to his success. Cyrus created the Persian Empire because he was a brilliant general who learned from his enemies. He also treated the people he conquered well, so they would not think they had to fight to the death against him. Instead, Cyrus took the soldiers he defeated and gave them jobs in his own army.

Cyrus started his conquests without a professional army. In order to build one, he took on the system of the Medes. That meant that he gave land to soldiers in

▼ **CYRUS THE GREAT**
This carving of Cyrus II from the ruins of an ancient Persian city shows him as a winged god.

CYRUS THE GREAT (CYRUS II) 559–529

575 B.C.

550 B.C.

547 Battle of Sardis

539 Persians invade Babylon.

525 B.C.

525 Cambyses invades Egypt.

exchange for their military support. He divided his army into units of 10, 100, 1,000, and 10,000 men to keep them under control. Organizing an army into units provided more structure than the Persians had before. Cyrus' troops admired him and trusted his leadership.

Even Cyrus' enemies thought well of him. When the Persians invaded Babylonia in 539 B.C., the Babylonians refused to fight for their own king. Instead, they opened the gates of their city and welcomed Cyrus.

DID YOU KNOW?

When Cambyses II, the son of Cyrus the Great, invaded Egypt in 525 B.C., an army of 50,000 of his men was killed by a desert sandstorm. Some historians and archaeologists think that story is a legend. Others still search for evidence of King Cambyses' lost army.

▼ **THE WALLS OF BABYLON**
The ruins of Babylon are one symbol of the past greatness of ancient civilizations in the Middle East. The walls of Babylon shown in this photograph were partly rebuilt by the former Iraqi president Saddam Hussein.

DARIUS THE GREAT (DARIUS I) 522–486	XERXES I 485–465		DARIUS III 336–330

500 B.C.
494 Battle of Miletus
490 Battle of Marathon

475 B.C.
480 Battles of Thermopylae, Salamis, and Cape Artemisium

300 B.C.
333 Battle of Issus
331 Battle of Gaugamela

Cyrus responded by releasing the Jews that were held captive there, and set in motion the world's first oath of human rights. He promised that all people in his empire would be treated as equals, no matter their race or religion.

Darius the Great

Darius I ruled from 522 to 486 B.C. His army was smaller than Cyrus', but more skilled. Darius improved the way the empire was organized and managed. He encouraged trade and commerce to make his empire richer.

Darius built a new capital at Persepolis, improved roads, and dug canals. He introduced a universal system of weights and measures. He also standardized gold and silver coins, and started a banking system. Darius built strong relationships with kingdoms outside the empire, just as he maintained peace within it.

But Darius was not as admired as Cyrus had been. He led a quiet life, and distanced himself from other people, even his advisers. Darius trusted few people to lead his army. Like the kings who came after him, he

◄ THE CYRUS CYLINDER
The writing on this cylinder is a statement by Cyrus the Great granting equal rights to the Babylonians he had just conquered. Because it shows that Cyrus respected human rights even in time of war, a copy of the cylinder is displayed at the headquarters of the United Nations in New York City.

depended on relatives—whether they understood war tactics or not.

Darius did not conquer new lands as Cyrus the Great had, but he held territory already under Persian control. He put down rebellions in Babylonia, for instance. Darius' most difficult challenge came when the Greeks under his power in western Asia rebelled. Greek soldiers from mainland Greece supported the rebels, and it took years of fighting to defeat them. But Darius managed well. He discovered that the Persian cavalry could defeat the Greeks as long as they fought on even ground. Darius also organized an enormous **fleet** that defeated the Greek rebels at sea.

In Their Own Words

"All the kingdoms of the earth the Lord, the God of heaven, has given to me, and he has also charged me to build him a house in Jerusalem, in Judah. Whoever, therefore, among you belongs to any part of his people, let him go up, and may his God be with him!"

—Cyrus the Great allowing the Jews to return from their exile in Babylon, as recounted in the Old Testament, 3rd–4th century B.C.

▼ **DARIUS I ON HIS THRONE**
In this sculpture, a high official pays **homage** to King Darius I. The Persian court performed great ceremonies that honored the king.

CHAPTER 5

War at Sea

The Persian **navy** became the most successful part of its military. That was because the Persians had won a ready-made navy when they conquered the Phoenicians in 539 B.C. The Persians divided Phoenician territory into four **vassal** kingdoms.

Before being conquered, the Phoenicians had thrived on the east coast of the Mediterranean Sea for centuries. During that time they became excellent naval warriors. Still, the Phoenicians were no match for the Persians. The Persians absorbed the Phoenicians into their empire and instantly became a major sea power.

The Trireme

Most warships in the Persian fleet were **triremes**. Those supported three levels of rowers, or about 200 men. Smaller ships with two levels of rowers were known as **biremes**. Triremes were the fastest warships of the ancient world. They moved swiftly and were easy to control. Each trireme had a weapon called a ram—a great iron beam that stuck out front under the waterline. The aim of trireme fighting was to smash into the enemy's ship. Once an enemy ship was hit, it was possible for **marines** to leap onboard and fight in close combat.

The ship was steered with a long steering oar.

Marines sat or even lay on the flat deck as the ship went into battle.

▲ GREEK BIREME
A bireme was similar to a trireme but had only two banks of oars rather than three. The ship itself, with its huge bronze ram at the **bow**, was the main weapon in war at sea.

The bronze ram below the waterline was sharp. It could rip a hole in an enemy ship.

Phoenician warships had masts and simple square sails. Sails were often left on shore when ships were going into battle. Ships were instead rowed into battle so soldiers did not have to rely on wind power to go from place to place.

Triremes were expensive, complex warships. They required skilled men to operate them. As a result, fighting at sea was different from fighting on land. On land, soldiers brought their own equipment. The Persians provided some training, but fighting methods were simple. At sea, it was the king who provided the ships. Men trained for months to learn how to row properly. It took even longer to learn how to fight well. Warfare at sea required a higher level of skill than fighting on land.

The Persians at Sea

Persian kings quickly realized that ships were highly useful. When Cambyses II conquered Egypt in 525 B.C., he had the support of the new Persian fleet. The fleet was even more useful against Greek rebels. The Persians defeated them in 494 B.C., in a major sea battle at Miletus, on the coast of western Anatolia (present-day Turkey). But the Persian fleet had some weaknesses. For instance, Phoenicians, Egyptians, and Greeks manned the ships. The only Persians onboard were marines—and few Persians knew how to swim.

But it was the Persian fleet that nearly won Greek territory when King Xerxes invaded that region in 480 B.C. Xerxes was determined to finish the work of his father Darius and defeat the Greeks. He came with a huge army and a fleet of more than 1,000 ships. The Greeks nearly stopped his foot soldiers at the battle of Thermopylae, when Greek armor proved so much better than that of the Persians. The Persian ships were high quality. But the fleet's great weakness was that the captains were not used to the waters off the coast of Greece. That lack of knowledge helped the Greeks win the battle of Salamis.

6 Watching the Defeat
The Persian King Xerxes, seated on a throne, watches from the shore as his great fleet is defeated and flees.

5 Greeks Turn on the Invaders
The Greeks turn and attack the disorganized Persian fleet.

1 A False Retreat
The Corinthians and other Greek ships lure the Persians into the narrow strait of Salamis by pretending to flee.

4 Persians in Chaos
Caught by the currents of the strait, the Persian ships are bunched together too tightly and cannot move easily to fight the attacking Greeks.

SALAMIS

Key

Greek ships

Persian ships

2 **Taking the Bait**
The Persian fleet follows the Greeks directly into the strait because they think the Greeks are escaping.

3 **A Surprise Attack**
Some Greek ships are hidden in a side bay. They attack the Persian fleet from the side, taking it by surprise.

The Battle of Salamis
480 B.C.

Many ships in the Persian fleet were destroyed in a storm. The fleet had also been hurt badly at the battle of Cape Artemisium (Ah-tem-ME-see-um) earlier that year. But the Persian fleet still outnumbered the Greek fleet when they met at the battle of Salamis. The battle took place in the strait of water between Piraeus (near Athens) and the island of Salamis.

Xerxes must have been confident of victory. His army had already destroyed Athens. He probably was not surprised when he received a message from a Greek traitor warning him that the Greek fleet would try to escape in the night. But the message was a trap. The Persian ships patrolled all night in vain, and the crews were tired when they finally saw the Greek fleet approaching. The Greeks then lured the Persians into a narrow channel and attacked them. The Greeks, who were skilled mariners and familiar with the waters, won a clever victory.

In close fighting on board ships, marines needed small weapons like this hand axe.

This marine also carries a small bow and arrows for longer-range fighting.

Marines used small shields because larger ones would be in the way on board a ship.

◄ **A PERSIAN MARINE**
Marines sat uncomfortably on the deck of each warship, ready to fight hand-to-hand with enemy crews when the ships made contact.

Fall of Empire

The Persian defeat at Salamis marked the fall of the Achaemenid Empire. Had the Persians conquered the Greeks, their empire may have lasted. Later, when Alexander the Great invaded Persia in 334 B.C., he defeated the Persians only by marching along the coast and taking Persian ports one-by-one. Slowly, Alexander's well-trained army defeated the Persians and took their territory. The Achaemenid Empire died with the death of Alexander's enemy Darius III.

Alexander himself died only a few years later, and his generals divided up the empire between them. The largest part included most of the Persian Empire. Its rulers transformed the Persian army. They settled Greek soldiers in cities throughout the empire, and trained the Persians to fight on foot in heavy armor like Greeks. Cavalry and archery gradually died out in Persia. This made it easy for the next invaders, the nomadic Parthians, who fought with arrows on horseback, to take over the region in 247 B.C.

▼ **WARSHIP ON THE NILE**
This mosaic from ancient Egypt shows a Persian warship going into battle packed with marines ready to attack. Persian influence was felt throughout the ancient world, including Africa.

Glossary

Achaemenid Empire—the area of Asia and North Africa ruled by the Achaemenid kings of Persia between 550 and 330 B.C.

akinakes—short, double-edged swords used by Persian warriors

Aramaic—an language which first developed in ancient Syria and was spoken throughout the Achaemenid Empire

archers—soldiers armed with bows and arrows

Babylonians—people who lived in the ancient city of Babylon, in present-day Iraq

barbarians—negative word for an uncivilized and inferior people

biremes—ships with two levels of rowers on each side

bow—the front of a ship

breastplates—pieces of armor worn on the chest to protect the heart and other organs

caravan—a group of people or an army traveling together, usually across a desert in Asia or North Africa

cavalry—soldiers who fight on horseback

compound bows—bows made from layers of wood, animal horn, and sinew

empire—a region or group of states under a single supreme authority or ruler

fleet—a group of ships under one commander

fortress—a well-defended military camp or fortified town occupied by soldiers

homage—public acknowledgment of respect or allegiance

javelins—light spears designed to be thrown by hand

Lydians—an ancient people from Lydia, an area in present-day Turkey

marines—soldiers trained to fight from and on board ships

Medes—an ancient people from the northwest of present-day Iran

navy—the part of a nation's armed forces that fights with ships at sea

nomads—people who choose to live with no permanent home, moving their posessions from place to place to find fresh pasture for their animals

quiver—a small case with a carrying strap, used for storing arrows

satrap—the governor of a Persian province

satrapies—provinces of ancient Persia

scythed chariot—a two-wheeled horsedrawn vehicle with swords fixed to the wheel axles

Silk Road—an ancient trading route across Asia that linked China with the Mediterranean Sea

slingers—soldiers trained to throw stones accurately using slings, lengths of rope with pouches in the middle

10,000 Immortals—an elite force of heavily armored Persian soldiers who guarded the king

triremes—ships with three levels of rowers on each side

tunic—a loose, sleeveless item of clothing reaching to the wearer's knees

vassal—a person or country in a subordinate position, ruled over by another

Zoroastrianism—a religion based on the teachings of the prophet Zoroaster, which flourished in the Middle East from around 500 B.C. to A.D. 650

For More Information

Books

Ancient Persia: A Myreportlinks.com Book. Civilizations of the Ancient World (series). Neil D. Bramwell (Enslow Publishers, 2004)

The Ancient Persians. Lost Civilizations (series). James Barter (Lucent Books, 2005)

Empire of Ancient Persia. Great Empires of the World (series). Micheal Burgan (Chelsea House Publishers, 2009)

Persian. Life During the Great Civilizations (series). Don Nardo (Blackbirch Press, 2003)

The Persian Empire. Lindsay Allen (University of Chicago Press, 2005)

The Persians: Warriors Of The Ancient World. Ancient Civilizations (series). Katherine Reece (Rourke Publishing, 2005)

You Wouldn't Want to Be an Assyrian Soldier!: An Ancient Army You'd Rather Not Join. You Wouldn't Want To… (series). Rupert Matthews (Children's Press, 2007)

Web Sites

EDSITEment's Persian Wars Resource Pages
http://edsitement.neh.gov/PersiaGreeceWars01.asp
Learn more about the battles fought between the ancient Persians and Greeks.

Forgotten Empire:
The World of Ancient Persia
http://www.thebritishmuseum.ac.uk/ forgottenempire
Discover unusual facts about the Persian Empire placed among photos of interesting ancient artifacts.

History of Iran: Achaemenid Empire
http://www.iranchamber.com/history/persepolis/ persepolis1.php
Explore the ruins of Persepolis, an ancient Persian city.

The Oriental Institute at the University of Chicago: Persepolis and Ancient Iran
http://oi.uchicago.edu/museum/collections/pa/ persepolis
Review the latest archaeological discoveries about ancient Persepolis.

Social Studies for Kids: Persian Wars
www.socialstudiesforkids.com/subjects/ persianwars.htm
Read about the wars between the ancient Persians and Greeks, including a time line and a map of the Persian Empire.

Publisher's note to educators and parents: Our editors have carefully reviewed these web sites to ensure that they are suitable for children. Many web sites change frequently, however, and we cannot guarantee that a site's future contents will continue to meet our high standards of quality and educational value. Be advised that children should be closely supervised whenever they access the Internet.

Index

About the Author

Dr. Phyllis G. Jestice is Assistant Professor of Medieval History at the University of Southern Mississippi. She was previously a Lecturer in Ancient and Medieval History at California State University. She is the author of sections of several other books including *Battles of the Ancient World* and *Battles of the Bible*.